Gospel-Centered Motherhood

STEFANIE BOYLES

Topics

BIBLICAL WOMANHOOD, LIKE
BIBLICAL MANHOOD, IS ROOTED
IN THE ULTIMATE CALLING FOR ALL
CREATION TO GLORIFY GOD.

A Woman's Highest Calling

What is a woman's highest calling? What is the value and purpose of women? Do these things vary between genders? Womanhood tends to be a contentious topic both inside and outside of the church. Some people glorify womanhood while others belittle it. More than ever, believers must go to the Word of God and ask, "What does Scripture say about the value and purpose of women?" Going to Scripture is the only way for women in the church to think biblically about womanhood.

From the very beginning, God declared equal value to human beings. Genesis 1:27 says, "So God created man in His own image; He created him in the image of God; He created them male and female." While there was gender distinctiveness, the value of each gender was tethered to the Creator because the value bestowed upon men and women was the image of God. And it is from this place of equal essence and value that we function in our distinct roles as men and women even today. In God's design, personhood precedes manhood and womanhood.

However, gender distinctiveness does exist. Our God is a God of order, and in an orderly way, He created the world according to His divine design. We see that God made Adam first, and then He made Eve as his helper (Genesis 2:18). In Scripture, a helper is not an inferior role. The same Hebrew word for "helper" that is used for Eve is used more often to describe God. Throughout the Old Testament, God is described as the helper of His people. In the New Testament, the Holy Spirit is called the helper. Women were created to image God by taking the posture of a helper, and this posture can be lived out by all women, single or married. The role of helper supports the biblical vision of men and women living and working in partnership as equals, complementing each other.

Biblical womanhood, like biblical manhood, is rooted in the ultimate calling for all creation to glorify God. As the Creator, God made all things to put His own glory on display. In Psalm 148, there is a call for collective praise of the Creator. Angelic beings, the sun and moon and stars, sea creatures, mountains and hills, animals, and all people are to praise the Lord. The way this purpose is fulfilled is for each created thing and being to be who the Creator made it to be. Dolphins glorify God by frolicking in the water. Mountains glorify God by standing majestically in the landscape. Wildflowers glorify God by blooming in due season. Women glorify God by being women just as men glorify God by being men.

God has equipped women to put His glory on display in many different ways. We are entrusted with different gifts for the edification of the body of Christ (1 Corinthians 12). We strive to put the image of Christ on display in our specific spheres of influence by pursuing Christlikeness. While men and women have unique ways of fulfilling the mandate to fill, subdue, and have dominion over the earth (Genesis 2), they do it together with the ultimate goal of putting God's glory on display. That is a woman's highest calling.

SCRIPTURE TO MEDITATE ON

Genesis 1:27, Psalm 148:11-13

What have you deemed as your highest calling in life? How has that impacted the way you spend your time, energy, talents, and resources? Take some time to confess any misunderstandings you may have about womanhood, and ask the Lord to help you put God's glory on display.

THE HOLY CALLING OF
MOTHERHOOD HAS THE ULTIMATE
AIM OF GLORIFYING CHRIST.

Motherhood is a Calling

The highest calling of a woman is not motherhood. Her highest calling is to glorify God. However, motherhood is still a calling. It is a high and holy calling. When we look at Scripture, we see that families are greatly valued. While there is no preferential treatment based on gender when it comes to our union with Christ, we can see that there is a design and order that God has instituted in His Word. And in this design, it is evident that women (and those who are called to be mothers) are held in high esteem. This is contrary to our culture's opinion of motherhood, which holds a very narrow view. Raising children is deemed a socially devalued venture—a highly demanding job with little return. Home management is seen as trivial, and new ways to outsource this particular work are presented every day.

Biblical motherhood is not defined by whether or not a woman works inside or outside of the home. It goes beyond behavior. The holy calling of motherhood has the ultimate aim of glorifying Christ. It is a high calling because motherhood is an incredibly potent means of grace. Think about it: moms have the opportunity to pass on a legacy of grace from one generation to the next. They are ambassadors of Christ in the home and the lives of their children. In and through this role, mothers have the opportunity to pass on a God-centered worldview. This transmission of beliefs, values, and worldview happens regardless of our intentions. The way we tend to the needs and cares of our families communicates and teaches these foundational truths. The way we live, our functional theology, says a lot more about our formal theology than what we say.

So much of the soul-shaping part of parenthood happens in the unplanned moments when we simply are who we are. So we have to ask ourselves—Who are we? Are we in Christ? Do our thoughts, words, and deeds align with being redeemed children of God? Does the way we extend grace testify to the fact that we are recipients of God's extravagant grace? Are we exhibiting joyful submission to the lordship of Christ in our lives through obedience to His Word? Is the gospel really good news to us, bringing us joy, strength, peace, and comfort? Parents have ample opportunities to display the gospel within the four walls of their homes.

Yet, when it comes to sharing the gospel, many of us think about people outside our homes. We think about our unsaved neighbors and co-workers. We can feel a deeper sense of purpose when the work of our hands benefits those outside our homes, which can cause some of us to be more eager to serve beyond our four walls. Some of us struggle to find deep satisfaction and value in serving the people within our homes. Why is that? Are we forgetting that our children are our neighbors too? Do we overlook the truth that they are image-bearers of God with intrinsic worth because their small frames are reliant on us, day in and day out?

The more we see our children as our neighbors, the more we will see motherhood as a worthy calling. We will see our homes as a mission field for the kingdom of God. We will be more intentional in creating a gospel-saturated culture through our thoughts, words, and deeds. We will see Scripture overflowing with instruction on how to raise our kids for His glory. May we eliminate the discrepancy between how we speak and treat the people in our neighborhood and how we treat those inside our home. May we strive to always be faithful ambassadors of Christ.

SCRIPTURE TO MEDITATE ON

Ephesians 5:1-2, Matthew 22:37-40

How do you adorn the gospel in your everyday life? Do you see your children as your neighbors? How would seeing your children as your neighbors impact the way you parent? Take some time to pray. Confess any sins if necessary.

BEING IN GOD'S WORD
IS FOR EVERY SEASON,
WITHOUT EXCEPTION.

In His Word in Every Season

A popular phrase employed by many individuals both inside and outside of the church is, "It's not my season." This phrase is often used as a blanket explanation for some sort of limitation in our lives. Maybe we are in the haze of newborn days and cannot prepare homemade meals every evening. Maybe we are in college and cannot afford to go out to eat with friends as often as we are invited. Maybe we are taking care of aging parents and cannot volunteer in the church in the way we would like. We feel as if we cannot do everything all the time—and rightfully so. God, in His infinite wisdom, made us as finite beings with limitations for our good.

But we have to be careful not to extend this idea to our personal time in the Word of God. Being in God's Word is for every season, without exception. It may look different in various seasons of life, but for all believers, it is the source of daily sustenance. Jesus said in Matthew 4:4, "Man shall not live by bread alone, but by every word that comes from the mouth of God." The Apostle Paul said that when receiving the law, Moses was receiving "living oracles to give to us" (Acts 7:38). The Bible holds the living words of God, and His words alone have the power to truly nourish, sustain, and strengthen us, day in and day out.

Motherhood is hard. Every season has its challenges. When our kids are babies and toddlers, we are physically taxed. We may not sleep through the night. We may not be able to prepare nutritious meals for ourselves, exercise, or even get showered and ready for the day. Our young ones need help with every aspect of daily living. However, as they grow, their needs change. Though the physical demands may diminish, the emotional, mental, and spiritual needs heighten. We may tell ourselves that the next season of motherhood will include a margin for pursuing spiritual growth, but the truth is, busyness is not the barrier to holiness. The real barrier is unbelief.

We are never too busy for what we deem as truly valuable. So we have to ask ourselves if we believe the Bible is worth our time and effort. Do we see "wondrous things from [His] instruction" (Psalm 119:18) so much so that we are compelled to discipline ourselves in the reading and studying of His Word? Our priorities, no matter our season of life, are ordered by the affections of our hearts. So what do we accomplish every single day without fail? Perhaps those things are most telling of what the greatest affections of our hearts truly are.

We can have the best intentions to disciple our children in the Lord. We can filter what they are exposed to, diligently take them to church and pray with them before every meal, and encourage them to read the Bible for themselves. But do our children see us faithfully feasting on His Word? Do our children see us going to His Word, day in and day out, and finding it to be the ultimate source of our joy, strength, and purpose in life? Or do they see us running on fumes, pulling ourselves up by our bootstraps to get through the day?

Mamas, we need to tend to our children's needs. It is also important for us to acknowledge our limitations through each season of life. However, may we never buy into the lie that there are seasons when daily Bible intake is unnecessary or unattainable. Instead, may we confess that we cannot do motherhood apart from His daily provision of grace, mercy, and empowerment. May we live as if His Word sustains our souls much like food sustains our physical bodies, and may we grow in holiness to be the vessels of His grace we are called to be in the lives of our children.

SCRIPTURE TO MEDITATE ON

2 Timothy 3:16-17, Psalm 19:7-11

QUESTIONS TO CONSIDER TO PROMPT PRAYER

Do you believe the Word of God is nourishment to your soul? What role does the Word of God play in your day to day living? Do you find yourself depending on God to make it through the day or relying on yourself instead? Take some time to pray. Confess any sins if necessary.

OUR CHILDREN ARE LOOKING AT
THE WHOLE OF OUR LIVES—WORDS
AND DEEDS—TO SEE WHAT WE
DEEM AS VALUABLE AND TRUE.

Discipleship in the Home

Discipleship can be an unfamiliar concept to many people. It can sound intimidating, and we may view it as something only pastors and seminary graduates do. However, the call to engage in discipleship is for all followers of Christ. Every disciple is called to make disciples. This is God's plan for the expansion of His kingdom here on earth. Jesus's charge, "Go, therefore, and make disciples of all nations, baptizing them in the name of the Father and of the Son and of the Holy Spirit, teaching them to observe everything I have commanded you," is for all Christians (Matthew 28:19-20).

This includes any mom who professes to follow Jesus as her Lord and Savior. It is so easy for us to see the harvest outside the four walls of our homes, but our families are eternal souls in need of the gospel too. Our children are our primary neighbors, and to love these very neighbors as ourselves, we must share the good news of the gospel with them. In our roles as moms, we have ample opportunities to display the gospel. This is why motherhood is a holy calling.

Discipleship in the home is most often organic. There can be formal elements like a morning time or family worship, which would include Bible reading, a devotional, and prayer. However, all of the mundane moments of life can be opportunities to disciple our children because they are opportunities to emulate the life and purpose of Jesus. Jesus was self-giving. He walked toward those in hard circumstances. He embodied the fruit of the Spirit; He was unwaveringly loving, joyful, peaceful, patient, kind, good, faithful, and gentle. He always exercised self-control. He was compassionate, and He proclaimed the gospel to those around Him. As followers of Christ, we are to do the same. We are "clothed with Christ" (Galatians 3:27).

We need to do this, first and foremost, in our homes. And as moms, we need to see every moment as an opportunity to adorn the gospel—in the meals we prepare, in the diapers we change, in the laundry we wash and fold, in the books we read aloud, in the way we transport our kids from one activity to the next, and even in the way we balance work inside and outside the home. Often, we can see these tasks as things we have to do, so much so that if we are not careful, we can simply tend to a need and miss the heart. We can find ourselves operating in survival mode, moving from one job to the next. In doing so, we can miss the fertile grounds to establish heart connections with our children, which are powerful means to communicate the love and tender care of Christ.

We have to remember the saying that more is caught than taught. Our children are looking at the whole of our lives—words and deeds—to see what we deem as valuable and true. They see if we are going to the Word of God every day for strength and guidance. They are observing our attitude, tone of voice, coping mechanisms, and level of joy to see if the gospel is good news. So we have to ask, do our children see us in the Word? Do they see that it is the gospel bringing us joy?

SCRIPTURE TO MEDITATE ON

Matthew 28:19-20, Colossians 3:12-17

QUESTIONS TO CONSIDER TO PROMPT PRAYER

When you read the Great Commission, do you read it as a call for you to make disciples? What does discipleship look like in your home? How can you grow more in Christlikeness? Take some time to pray. Confess any sins if necessary.

"

The more we see
our children as our
neighbors, the more
we will see motherhood
as a worthy calling.

WHEN WE GIVE OF OURSELVES TO
OUR SPOUSES AND CHILDREN,
WE ARE REFLECTING CHRIST AND
HIS SELF-GIVING LOVE.

Dying to Self is the Way to Joy

Motherhood is messy. Children are not always obedient. Sickness usually comes and goes, but for some, it is a permanent reality. There are countless stressors—finances, educational choices, home management needs, multiple schedules, and the list goes on. Furthermore, there are natural growing pains that come with changing life seasons. And despite how much we love our families, we know our children are not perfect, our spouses are not perfect, and we are not perfect. This is a universal reality of our fallen nature. Parents and children alike are sinners in need of a Savior. We need Jesus! But we also cannot forget that our union with Christ does not transport us to a perfectly ordered world and life. Though we are declared positionally righteous in Christ, we are still in the process of being redeemed on this side of heaven.

Regarding the Christian life, Jesus says in Matthew 7:14, "How narrow is the gate and difficult the road that leads to life, and few find it." Yet, if we are honest, so many of us are confused when we encounter any sort of hardship in our lives. We get easily disheartened when any degree of suffering or discomfort comes. We may even wonder if it is a direct result of some level of disobedience in our hearts. What did Jesus mean when He said the way to life is narrow and hard? And what implications does this have for our journeys through motherhood?

Jesus was closing His teaching on the Sermon on the Mount (Matthew 5-7). His conclusion included a call to true faith and salvation. He was drawing the line between two ways of living—one way leads to eternal life, and the other leads to eternal damnation. The narrow way is hard because it involves completely trusting in the person and work of Christ for righteousness. It requires submitting to His lordship. This way of life involves regular repentance and the mortification of the sinful tendencies in our lives with the help of the indwelling Spirit. We are surrendering our desires for His desires and striving to obey His commands, no matter the cost. Apart from the Lord's grace and power, we would be unable to do any of this. Salvation is a gift provided by saving grace, and we continue to live in light of the resurrection only by His sustaining grace.

What does this mean for motherhood? Should we expect it to be a difficult journey? Our culture perpetuates the message that motherhood is messy and hard. It characterizes the calling of motherhood as one sacrificing physical beauty, sleep, uninterrupted work, conveniences, freedom, cleanliness, finances, and more. And it is true to some degree. Motherhood is hard. We are entrusted with wholly caring for other people, and this requires work. We do find ourselves expending physical, mental, and emotional energy to varying degrees, depending on our season of motherhood. However, hard does not mean bad. It does not mean wrong or undesirable. It is not void of tremendous value. For believers, motherhood is an invitation to grow in godliness which ultimately leads to God's glory and our good.

And here is the truth about walking the narrow way and being united to Christ: it is the way to life. Jesus said that He came so that we may "have life and have it in abundance" (John 10:10). He is "the way, the truth, and the life" (John 14:6). In His presence is the fullness of joy (Psalm 16:11), and His grace is sufficient for us (2 Corinthians 12:9). He supplies new mercies every morning, and His love is steadfast (Lamentations 3:22-23). In our weakness, His strength is readily available to sustain and empower us (2 Corinthians 12:10). Motherhood and all of its unseen work is holy work that has eternal value if it is done unto the Lord!

God has ordered things in such a way that our happiness is exponentially multiplied when we love and serve others for the glory of God. When we give of ourselves to our spouses and children, we are reflecting Christ and His self-giving love. In God's economy, when His people empty themselves for His sake, they are filled with His presence which leads to purpose, joy, and satisfaction. The call to follow Christ by denying ourselves and picking up our crosses every day is the call to finding eternal delight.

QUESTIONS TO CONSIDER TO PROMPT PRAYER

Is it difficult for you to reconcile the truth that dying to self is the way to joy? What would dying to self look like in your life? How would that increase your joy in the Lord? Take some time to pray. Confess any sins if necessary.

WE MUST HAVE A FIRM
UNDERSTANDING OF GOD'S
VISION FOR MARRIAGE AND DO
WHATEVER IS NECESSARY TO
LIVE IN LIGHT OF THAT VISION.

Guarding Our Marriages

The demands of motherhood can be overwhelming. It does not matter how many children we have under our care or what their ages and stages are—the needs abound. They require our time and energy to tend to these very needs. This is why marriages are undeniably changed when children enter the picture. While our hearts seem to expand with love as our families grow, time remains fixed, and we remain limited beings required to operate within the confines of our God-given boundaries.

This is why it is of utmost importance that we seriously consider ways to guard our marriages. Whether we are in the throes of parenthood yet or not, we must have a firm understanding of God's vision for marriage and do whatever is necessary to live in light of that vision. With children, changes will come. Family dynamics, responsibilities, and even hopes and dreams will change. But through it all, we cannot forget the sanctity of marriage set forth by God. In marriage, a husband and wife are one. They are bound together in a covenant relationship, and marriage is to be a picture of the unbreakable covenant between Christ and the Church. No matter how a family grows or changes, the sacred commitment between a husband and his wife remains. We are not in covenant relationships with our children. While we do offer self-giving love and care to our children, it should not come at the expense of the sacrificial love and care we give to our spouses.

Yet, this is hard to live out in reality. It can be difficult to manage the increasing needs and demands of family life when our time, energy, and resources are limited. We cannot do it all and do it well. So we have to be proactive, creative, and flexible, all while keeping our priorities straight. We may not be able to plan perfectly for future seasons of life, but we can be intentional in linking arms with our spouses in such a way that we can weather whatever the seasons may bring. Because the truth is, every season of mother-hood will pose different challenges to marriage. It is a myth that the younger years are more demanding and the older years. We cannot expect our marriages to thrive in any season without proper care and attention. We need to put safeguards in place.

We should protect our marriages by striving for consistent inti-macy. The truth is, time, energy, and desire for intimacy with our spouses will ebb and flow. However, this intimacy must be guarded and nurtured. This intimacy goes beyond sex, but it does include sex. Sex is sacred, and it is an exclusive gift given to a husband and his wife. While it is the primary means to procreate by God's design, He has also allowed it to be a means to experience deep intimacy, pleasure, love, and unity between a man and a woman in the context of marriage. It is not the greatest source of satisfaction in our lives, but it is a significant means to point us to the One who is. This level of physical intimacy affects our hearts, and it should be prioritized no matter our season of life. It is with good reason that the Apostle Paul set forth this principle for marriage in 1 Cor-inthians 7:4 when he said, "Do not deprive one another—except when you agree for a time, to devote yourselves to prayer. Then come together again; otherwise, Satan may tempt you because of your lack of self-control."

We also need to create a margin to tend to this relationship in oth-er ways. Perhaps this means investing in a new hobby that can be done together. Maybe this is committing to weekly date nights. We can get creative in making space to talk, laugh, and enjoy each other. We can reclaim the little moments of our days, and we can do this with kids around. We should seek to get to know each other better by asking intentional questions. We should establish healthy daily and weekly rhythms to allow for time and space to do this. The childrearing years may be full of needs that require your time, attention, energy, finances, and more; however, they can also be fertile ground for building a strong marriage.

Investing in our marriages is a tremendous way to invest in our children, our families, and our society as a whole. Our marriages are meant to put the gospel on display. They are meant to be a tangible representation of the steadfast love, devotion, and unity between Christ and the church. As spouses, we must extend grace to each other to weather the changes, and in doing so, we are also cultivating a gospel-saturated culture in our home.

SCRIPTURE TO MEDITATE ON

Genesis 2:24, Ephesians 5:22-26

How have the dynamics in your marriage changed after having kids? Are there any adjustments you need to make to better put the gospel on display through your marriage? Take some time to pray. Confess any sins if necessary.

*As spouses, we must
extend grace to each other
to weather the changes,
and in doing so, we are
also cultivating a
gospel-saturated culture
in our home.*

WHEN YOU FEEL LIKE NO ONE ELSE
SEES YOUR TIRELESS EFFORTS,
REMEMBER THAT OUR GOD IS THE
GOD WHO SEES.

Encouragement for Single Moms

You are an image-bearer of God. This is where your value is found—in your Maker. If you have put your faith in Christ, you are united to Him, and your union with Christ is an imperishable gift. Your identity in Him transcends whatever has happened, is happening, and will happen in your life. Though each of our stories is different, every detail is known and seen by God. And each of us is invited to pursue Christlikeness, be transformed by His grace, and be used for His glory in our lives and our motherhood journeys.

Your story is your own, and it is not a mistake. Every single mom is where she is for different reasons. Some are divorced, and many different situations can lead to a dissolved marriage. Some are widows, and some may have never married. Ultimately, the details of our stories are our own, and what is most important is to remember that the Lord is in the business of redemption and restoration. This is true for all moms, single or married. Trust that He will finish the good work He started in you (Philippians 1:6).

Despite these truths, we know that single moms have been recipients of all sorts of judgment and assumptions, inside and outside of the church. However, the heart of Christ remains unchanged. He is gentle and lowly, and His love extends to His people, regardless of their marital status. In response, the Church—as the body of Christ—ought to extend tender love and care with impartiality, welcoming and serving single moms in their congregations, neighborhoods, and beyond.

If you are a single mom, here is some encouragement on your motherhood journey:

— *You are seen.* —

No one else may know your story, but we acknowledge the fact that the hardships of motherhood are compounded because you do not have a spouse to help you offset the load. You are responsible all the time. You need to provide financially and tend to you and your children physically, emotionally, mentally, and spiritually. You do this with no immediate relief or respite in sight. The exhaustion can be debilitating at times, and yet you have to press on. You likely experience a range of intense emotions—loneliness, fear, exhaustion. Just like any other mom, you desire the best for your children. As a follower of Christ, you want to share the gospel in word and deed with your children. You hope to raise them in such a way that the Word of God would dwell richly in them. This is a beautiful and eternally worthy vision of motherhood! When you feel like no one else sees your tireless efforts, remember that our God is the God who sees (Genesis 16:13).

— You are doing a great job. Keep going. —

Continue to be an ambassador of Christ in your home. You are an instrument in the hands of the Redeemer, and you are being used to shape your children. Trust in His able hands to use you and sustain you. Seek out a local body of believers who will run alongside you in this vision of raising disciples. You are not alone. A huge way the Lord provides for His people is through His people. The local church is your community. These people are imperfect, and they will not always say what is helpful. However, they can remind you of gospel truths when you forget. They can encourage you, pray for you, counsel you (if desired), and meet your practical needs. The body of Christ is commanded to "carry one another's burdens" (Galatians 6:2). They have gifts that you need, and you have gifts that they need.

— Jesus is enough. —

God is faithful to fill in the gaps. You may not have a husband with whom to be intimate, but praise God, the Lord calls Himself your husband and longs for intimacy with you (see Isaiah 54:5). Your children may not have an immediate fatherly figure to engage with, but praise God, they have a heavenly Father who is near and accessible in Christ. God is your Redeemer, and He can give you the wisdom, strength, joy, tenacity, and comfort you need to be faithful to what He has called you to this day. He is actively working in you, "both to will and to work for His good purpose" (Philippians 2:13). He is your Provider, and He will never forsake you. He welcomes all of you. Like David, you can pray, "Listen to my words, Lord; consider my sighing. Pay attention to the sound of my cry" (Psalm 5:1-2). He promises to draw near to those who seek Him.

Ultimately, remember that God is sovereign. He ordains all things for "the good of those who love God" (Romans 8:28). Surrender to Him. Allow His Spirit to strengthen your inner being. Abide in Christ, and be firmly anchored in His love. Seek Him in His Word. Trust that He is after your holiness and happiness. No matter your story, His grace is sufficient for you. Through your highs and lows, remember the enduring hope you have in Christ, and allow that to sustain you as you lament and praise on your journey.

SCRIPTURE TO MEDITATE ON

2 Corinthians 12:9-10, Psalm 138:8

QUESTIONS TO CONSIDER TO PROMPT PRAYER

Are you weary today? Where are you looking for strength and reprieve? How can you depend on God and His people as you continue on this motherhood journey? Take some time to pray for yourself, and then take some time to pray for your children, entrusting them to Him.

*No matter your story,
His grace is sufficient for
you. Through your highs
and lows, remember the
enduring hope you have
in Christ, and allow
that to sustain you as
you lament and praise
on your journey.*

AS FOLLOWERS OF CHRIST, WE
ARE INVITED TO FIND AND ANCHOR
OUR IDENTITIES IN HIM.
THIS CHANGES EVERYTHING.

07

The Heart Issue Behind Mom Guilt

Motherhood is full of decisions to make, and these decisions have widespread effects. Sometimes, this reality can feel like a heavy burden. We want to do what is best, but we are aware of our limitations. Sometimes, finances limit us. Or maybe it is a lack of information, forethought, or energy. Many times, however, it is our sinful nature. We are sinners in need of God's sustaining grace every single day. Apart from Him, we can do nothing (John 15:5).

Yet, we often neglect to rely on His grace, wisdom, and strength in our mothering. Instead, we look to ourselves despite our insufficiencies and weaknesses. In the process, we increase the pressure on ourselves, and we find ourselves coming face to face with this thing called mom guilt. Mom guilt is familiar to most of us. It is the feeling that comes when we fail to meet our own expectations in parenting. We were not as patient as we hoped we would be. We did not notice the fever earlier. Our frustration led us to speak with a harsh tone. We cannot afford to buy our kids the latest trendy clothes. We did not start them in that sport or instrument earlier. We are not reading to them enough, laughing with them enough, playing with them enough. In short, mom guilt tells us we are not good enough. It tells us that we are failing our kids and need to pull up our bootstraps and try harder.

What does the gospel have to say about mom guilt? First, in and of itself, guilt is not bad. If we have sin in our lives, it is right for us to feel guilty. Encountering guilt in response to sin is a mercy because it is an invitation to repent. If we yell at our children out of unrighteous anger, we should feel guilt. The Spirit convicts us of our sin and beckons us to repent and find restoration. If we are exasperated with our children because they are not performing at the level of speed we would prefer, we would be right for feeling guilty because we are putting our comforts and conveniences before their needs and hearts. In repenting of our sins, we are posturing ourselves to be forgiven and transformed into Christ-likeness.

However, not all mom guilt is in response to sin in our lives. Sometimes, it is due to inappropriate expectations we place on ourselves as moms. We are limited creatures by God's good design. We cannot do and be everything for our children. So we have to ask what is shaping our expectations as moms. Are we looking to motherhood for our self-worth? Are we looking to our children to define our purpose? Have we employed our children to be the measuring stick of our faithfulness to God? Are we looking to our culture to set the bar of success in our parenting? Where are we finding our identity?

The truth is, the heart behind mom guilt is a misplaced identity. Yes, we are setting unrealistic expectations for ourselves which ensures that we will fall short and wrestle with guilt. However, it is our identities that inform the expectations and guidelines we set for ourselves. If our identities are found in motherhood, we will continually find ourselves swinging on the pendulum between insecurity and pride. We will look to the world around us to shape our standards and goals in motherhood. We will seek out the latest research about best parenting practices instead of looking to Scripture. We will continue to just try harder the next time rather than falling to our knees in prayer. We will look at our children's behavior to determine if we are a good mom. We will evaluate our children's successes and failures and equate their performance as our own success or failure as moms.

But there is a better way. As followers of Christ, we are invited to find and anchor our identities in Him. This changes everything. In Christ, we are saints, free from condemnation, eternally alive, new creations, justified, sanctified, and glorified. Our identities are not based on what we have done or will do but wholly on what God has done and what He will bring to completion. Our identities do not come from within ourselves but from outside of ourselves in the person and work of Christ. Our identities are founded on the eternal promises of God. When we anchor our identity in Him, we experience freedom from mom guilt because Jesus is the solution to all of our guilt. We acknowledge that we are sinners in need of His sustaining grace. We confess that we are not mom enough, and we rest in Christ who is enough. In a world full of mommy wars that can be toxic and cause us to drown in mom guilt, may we preach the gospel to ourselves and anchor our identities in Christ alone.

SCRIPTURE TO MEDITATE ON

Ephesians 1:7-14, John 15:16

QUESTIONS TO CONSIDER TO PROMPT PRAYER

When do you feel mom guilt? Is the reason due to sin or to misplaced identity? How would your finding identity in Christ impact the expectations you have for yourself as a mom? Take some time to pray. Confess any sins if necessary.

We are limited creatures
by God's good design.
We cannot do and
be everything for our
children. So we have to
ask what is shaping our
expectations as moms.

THESE YEARS ARE FORMATIVE,
NOT JUST FOR THE ONES IN
OUR CARE, BUT FOR OUR SOULS.

Encouragement for the Little Years

Before we even become mothers, we are bombarded with decisions. We are encouraged to have a birth plan. Do we opt for a home birth, natural birth, midwife, doctor, doula, epidural, IV medications, induction, or cesarean? What will our plan be for birth control after the baby? Are we going to breastfeed or bottle-feed? Then when the baby is born, the questions continue. If we breastfeed, when should we stop? If we bottle-feed, what formula should we use? Do we use pacifiers? How do we sleep-train? Do we co-sleep? What about our careers? Do we work inside or outside the home? Do we work part-time or full-time?

These decisions can feel daunting, and it does not help that these are now contentious issues in our culture. If we are not careful, we can lose sight of the tremendous gift of life entrusted to our care before they are even in our arms. And the battle of delighting in our children continues, especially in the younger years. These are the years that are demanding of our whole selves. Our children rely on us for everything. We are physically, emotionally, mentally, and spiritually stretched. It can feel like we are in the trenches of motherhood. There may be many days when it feels like we are running in place (maybe even falling behind!). These years when children are little are undoubtedly hard. However, these years are formative, not just for the ones in our care, but for our souls.

The little years matter. God has designed our children's brains to be incredibly formidable. Scientists say millions of neural connections are made at a rapid rate in the early years, and these connections are influenced by a variety of things like a child's interactions with other people, his or her environment, and more. As mothers, we have the opportunity to be one of the greatest influences in our children's lives and profoundly impact which connections are being made. We do not have the power to demand who our children will be; however, we can be instruments in the hands of our Redeemer in shaping who our children are becoming day by day.

This can be done by curating a gospel-saturated culture in our homes. As we teach our children to follow rules, ask for forgiveness, be generous and kind and loving, and more, we can proclaim the gospel. We follow rules because God's Word tells us that boundaries are for our good. But we know that we cannot follow all of the rules perfectly all the time—we need Jesus. And so we ask for forgiveness, knowing that God forgives us in Christ, and we ask for help to fight our sins. We are generous, kind, and loving in response to our God who is generous, kind, and loving. We are His image-bearers, and we are called to put His character on display. And this begins with us, as moms. The opportunities we have to put the character of God on display are endless. Our tone of voice, our choice of words, our decisions, our comforts and delights, our frustrations—all of these things communicate something about God to our children. As we share the gospel with our words, we can show how the gospel changes everything by the way we live. Our young children are observing everything whether we like it or not.

These little years can feel void of fruit, but we must not underestimate the value of consistency and repetition. Even in our discipline efforts, may we not grow weary and be blinded to the progress and growth that the Lord is working in our children. As for the countless decisions we have to make, may we find peace in knowing that many of them fall into the gray areas of Scripture. The Bible offers us sufficient principles to guide us in our parenting journeys, but it is not strictly prescriptive. God has given His people the gift of personal conscience to help navigate these gray areas. We must submit our personal conscience to the Word of God by diligently studying it and allowing it to inform and shape our consciences. We can also seek counsel from older, Bible-believing sisters. We can pray and ask for the Spirit's help. And then, we can feel freedom in making decisions aligning with our consciences. As followers of Christ, we strive to stay faithful to Scripture, and we teach our children to do the same (Deuteronomy 6). Motherhood in these little years is particularly sanctifying as we are frequently confronted with our own sinful inclinations. However, we can lean on the grace and strength of God. His grace is sufficient, and His power is made perfect in our weakness (2 Corinthians 12:9).

SCRIPTURE TO MEDITATE ON

Psalm 127:3, Mark 10:13-16

QUESTIONS TO CONSIDER TO PROMPT PRAYER

*Do you find yourself longing for a future season? What small thing
could you do today to delight in your young children? What is a simple
way you can help your child know God? Take some time to pray.
Confess any sins if necessary.*

"

We do not have the power to demand who our children will be; however, we can be instruments in the hands of our Redeemer in shaping who our children are becoming day by day.

OUR CHILDREN NEED THE GOSPEL
AT EVERY AGE, AND IT IS OUR
MISSION TO COMMUNICATE THE
TRUTHS FOUND IN SCRIPTURE.

09

Encouragement for the Older Years

Some of us look longingly to future seasons. Maybe we are in the thick of diapers or tantrums or puberty, and we think that things will get easier when our children are older. This is when it is helpful to hear the perspective of those who have already walked the future seasons. Though we may not want to hear it, the general message we may receive from those who have gone before us is that it does not get easier. Every season has its highs and lows. There will be joys and challenges every step of the way, and this is true regardless of the cultural climate that exists during the time we are parenting.

While it is certain that times are changing, human nature and its bent toward sin have not changed. Ever since the fall, the world has been hostile to God and what He deems as good and true. The devil remains the father of lies, and his purpose continues to be deception (John 8:44). While research shows that teenagers are dramatically different than teens of decades past (primarily due to the rise in technology), heart issues remain the same. This is why the essential elements of parenting do not change too drastically throughout the seasons. Our children need the gospel at every age, and it is our mission to communicate the truths found in Scripture.

As in previous seasons, our older children need to know they are known and loved. We do not want to assume we know all of our older children's struggles. Instead, we should strive to be students of our children. We want to be active listeners. This may mean leaving a margin at the end of long days to welcome deeper conversations. This may require us to be better at asking intentional questions. We want to pay attention to their words, knowing words offer a glimpse into their hearts (Matthew 12:34). We want to be in tune with their emotions, knowing emotions reveal what one's heart believes to be true and valuable. Being a humble listener will communicate love, and it will position us to be able to help our older children apply the gospel to their personal needs and struggles.

Communicating with older children can feel like a delicate balance. We want to acknowledge the depravity of mankind yet embrace the inherent dignity of these image-bearers of God. We want to identify their sin patterns yet point them to the sufficiency of Christ. Ultimately, we want to magnify the beauty of the gospel. As parents, this requires us to adorn the gospel in real-time. Our actions and our words should reflect the freedom, hope, and peace we have in Christ. We should be joyful because that is the work of the Spirit of God in us. We want to communicate with our lives, day in and day out, that the gospel is not equivalent to moralism or legalism. The gospel is good news—it is freedom from the bondage of slavery and the joys of new life in Christ.

All of this can happen only in relationships with our children. Contrary to what our culture may tell us, our older children can be deeply delighted in and invested members of our families. When we put in the intentional effort to spend time with them, exchanging meaningful thoughts while sharing laughter and experiences, we are laying the groundwork for fruitful discipleship. Because that is the beauty of older children, that discipleship can be organic. We do life with our teens, incorporating rhythms that protect togetherness.

This does not mean we forfeit intentional times of exploring the Word of God together. As our children grow up and their attitudes change and their schedules fill up, we can be tempted to forego reading and memorizing Scripture together. But we cannot afford to do this. The Word of God is "living and active" (Hebrews 4:12). It convicts and comforts; it counsels and sanctifies; it shows us God's character and reveals our sin. More than our advice, we want to offer our older children the living Word of God, knowing it shows the way of salvation and abundant life. We can trust in the Word of God and the Spirit of God to reorder the affections of our children's hearts. We can trust Him to quench their deepest thirst. This can look different for every family. It does not have to be burdensome or dreadful, but rather a simple invitation to feast on God's Word alongside us.

In the end, there will undoubtedly be growing pains. Just like us, our children are sinners in need of a Redeemer. We may grow weary or feel disheartened, but may we hold fast to Christ. May we seek accountability and perspective from an older mentor who has already weathered the different seasons of motherhood. May we stay on our knees, fully dependent on the Lord, while extending open arms to our older children.

SCRIPTURE TO MEDITATE ON

James 1:5, James 1:19-20

QUESTIONS TO CONSIDER TO PROMPT PRAYER

When you think about the teenage years, what thoughts come to mind? What fears do you have about raising teens in this day and age? What are a few things you can do every day to cultivate deeper relationships with your older children? Take some time to pray. Confess any sins if necessary.

Contrary to what our culture may tell us, our older children can be deeply delighted in and invested members of our families.

MOTHERHOOD, LIKE THE
CHRISTIAN WALK, REQUIRES
A LONG-TERM VISION.

10

Perseverance

If motherhood were likened to a race, it would be an ultra-marathon. Yet, more than an ultra-marathon, the finish line in the journey of motherhood is not clearly defined. Most of us would agree that our roles as a mom do not cease when our children turn eighteen years old and leave the home for college or work. As our children grow, our roles simply change. If we want any chance of running this motherhood race well, we need to be equipped for the long haul. Many elements of long-distance running can help us in our motherhood journeys.

First, most runners do not decide on a whim to run ultra-marathons. Much training is required to even complete these races, and they need to be committed to the program. Likewise, we need to hold the appropriate mindset regarding our calling as moms. We need to be committed to being stewards. As we see in the Bible, stewardship is wholly focused on managing whatever has been entrusted to us in such a way as to please the One to which everything belongs. Biblical stewardship is not self-focused but God-focused. The aim is to please Him.

We should resolve to view motherhood through this lens of biblical stewardship. This will cause us to redefine success in our mothering. Rather than measuring our parenting success by our children's behavior or by their abilities, character, or compliance, we define it as faithfulness. Success is faithfulness to what God has placed before us. Whether we are entrusted with one child or six children, the goal is to take every opportunity to glorify God. Having this mindset will help us avoid finding our worth in motherhood or our children. Instead, it will be anchored in our union with Christ and His unchanging character. Furthermore, it will help us to keep going when the going gets tough. Just like some training days are defined by fatigue and discouragement, we will have days that are exhausting and disheartening. Motherhood is full of mundane moments, but having a godward mindset will bring eternal value to even these moments. And with the Spirit's help, we can be empowered to do the next right thing.

Second, all runners would agree that proper nutrition and adequate hydration are essential. You will not race well if you are looking to junk food for sustenance. Likewise, moms need to properly nourish themselves each day. We need to feast on the Word of God which is nourishment to our very souls. Yes, it is so much quicker to consume encouraging snippets on social media about the Bible, but in a sense, that is spiritual junk food that ultimately will fail to satisfy and sustain long-term. The Word of God alone is "inspired by God" and "living and effective" (2 Timothy 3:16-17, Hebrews 4:12). While secondary resources can be helpful, they become more harmful when they become substitutes for the primary resource. If we are pressed for time, we need to form the habit of going to Scripture directly, and we need to do this every single day no matter our particular life season.

Third, we need to incorporate rhythms of rest. Every good training program incorporates rest because it lends to longevity. We are finite beings with vulnerable frames. God created us this way for our good, and He instituted a weekly rhythm that included a day of rest called the Sabbath. The heart behind the Sabbath is not legalism, concerned primarily with adhering to ancient rules and regulations. Instead, it is an invitation to rest and be refreshed. It is admitting our dependence on God and choosing to trust in His provision. It is an opportunity to regularly preach the gospel to ourselves—we are not God. Our world does not depend on us. He is trustworthy, and we can rest in Him.

But how do we rest well as moms? Our culture promotes a very self-centered approach to rest under the label of self-care. But what does the Bible say? A biblical perspective of self-care is contrary to "me-time." It is not about treating ourselves because we worked hard and think we deserve it. Instead, engaging in self-care in a way that honors God is motivated by the desire to yield to God's design for us. We rest to better serve God and others. The aim is to be refreshed to pour out again and fulfill the countless commands in Scripture to love, to serve, to honor, to build up, to show hospitality, to teach, to extend kindness and encouragement, and many more to one another. Self-care is not selfish in this regard. It is practiced to be effective instruments of God in our particular spheres of influence. This is true even for moms whose primary work may be in the home discipling their children.

Motherhood, like the Christian walk, requires a long-term vision. Everyday faithfulness is the goal, and this can only be done in partnership with the indwelling Spirit and obedience to His Word. God's Word tells us to abide in Him, and we can do this by feasting on Scripture daily and regularly going to Him for rest and refreshment.

SCRIPTURE TO MEDITATE ON

1 Corinthians 9:24-27, Galatians 6:9

QUESTIONS TO CONSIDER TO PROMPT PRAYER

How do you define success in motherhood? How does viewing motherhood through the lens of stewardship encourage you? What can you do to incorporate rhythms of rest and prioritize self-care to better serve God and others? Take some time to pray. Confess any sins if necessary.

Rather than measuring our parenting success by our children's behavior or by their abilities, character, or compliance, we define it as faithfulness. Success is faithfulness to what God has placed before us.

WHEN OUR CHILDREN SEE US
PRAY REGULARLY, THEY WILL
BETTER UNDERSTAND ITS VALUE.

11

Be a Praying Mom

Prayer may not come easily for many of us, but as moms, praying for our children probably feels effortless. When our babies are growing in the womb, we pray for healthy development. When they are born, we pray for peaceful sleep through the night. When they begin to walk, we pray for safety from bumps and bruises. When they are in school, we pray they would have wholesome friends and make wise choices. We may even pray for their salvation, future spouses, character, and other such things throughout the years. Praying for our children is good. It is truly one of the best gifts we can give our children.

Right after Jesus taught the Lord's prayer to His disciples in Luke 11, He shared a parable about a friend asking another friend for bread in the middle of the night. The principle in this parable is that we can persistently petition the Lord. We can and should bring the specific needs and desires of our children before the Lord. However, we do this with the understanding that God is sovereign and good. This means we pray, even if our prayers are not answered exactly how we want them to be or on a particular timeline. We pray because we are relating to God as our loving Father through the very act of prayer. We are entrusting our children to Him. We are yielding to the One who is ultimately in control. And the mystery in prayer is this: God uses the prayers of His people to accomplish what He has already willed to happen. Our prayers are purposeful and effective (James 5:16).

And prayer changes us. Praying helps us grow in godliness. Prayer changes us as it aligns us to God's will and His purposes. This happens as our intimacy with God grows. As we bring our needs before Him, we find His grace is sufficient. As we bring our brokenness before Him, we receive His comfort and healing. As we bring our sin before Him, we receive forgiveness and freedom. We are changed, and we are empowered by the Spirit to walk in obedience. This affects how we interact with our children. Any time we grow in Christlikeness, our children benefit for good because they can see a clearer picture of the God we image.

And while prayer is personal, we should also consider how we can model a praying life before our children. Our children observe everything we say and do. They see how we sweep up their crumbs after mealtime. They see us doing the laundry, getting the groceries, and driving around town. They assign value and importance to the things we consistently do. So we have to ask, do our children see us praying? Do they see us prioritize prayer? When our children see us pray regularly, they will better understand its value. When they see us rely on prayer for daily strength and grace and wisdom, they will not only get a glimpse of the power of prayer, but they will be reminded of the One who supplies all we need. When they see us cry before the Lord on behalf of others in need, they will see that God is the Comforter, Healer, and Provider. When we pray with or in front of our children, we are giving them the gift.

This is crucial because prayer is a spiritual discipline meant for all believers. In Scripture, we see that believers are commanded to "pray constantly" (1 Thessalonians 5:17). It is God's will for us to pray. But while it is a command, prayer is also very communal. As God speaks to us in His Word, we respond to Him in prayer. Prayer is a gift for God's people that was purchased at a high cost—the blood of Christ. When His grace and presence invade our hearts, we cannot help but respond in prayer. We want our children to see firsthand how a deep prayer life can and should be a natural outflowing of being a child of God. This does not mean that it is easy. We have to learn to pray, and we can begin by using the Lord's prayer as our framework (see Matthew 6 and Luke 11). If we feel at a loss for words, we can pray Scripture. Prayer is a discipline that can be cultivated, and it is a worthy pursuit with eternal implications for our children and ourselves.

SCRIPTURE TO MEDITATE ON

Luke 11:5-13, Matthew 6:7-13

QUESTIONS TO CONSIDER TO PROMPT PRAYER

What does your prayer life look like right now?
What does Jesus's parable in Luke 11 teach you about prayer?
Why is it important to engage in the spiritual discipline of prayer?
Take some time to pray. Confess any sins, if necessary.

WHEN IT COMES TO DISCIPLINE,
IT IS MORE HELPFUL TO CONSIDER
THE PRINCIPLES FOUND IN
SCRIPTURE THAN TO SEEK
A PRESCRIPTIVE APPROACH.

12

Discipline

God's Word instructs us that discipline is good. Scripture states in multiple places how the Lord disciplines those He loves (Proverbs 3:11-12, Hebrews 12:7-8). Discipline is an expression of love for His children because it is an investment in their spiritual growth. He does not abandon His people to their sinful nature, but He does what is necessary so that His people can share in His holiness (Hebrews 12:10). Likewise, we want to discipline our children in such a way that communicates that the discipline is motivated by our love seeking their ultimate good. We want love, not fear, to drive our children's obedience.

Discipline has and continues to be a touchy topic. Even within the church, there is not a universally accepted approach to the discipline of children. There are a handful of well-known verses that may come to mind when we think about this topic such as Proverbs 13:24, 22:15, and 23:13. These verses mention the use of a rod. Undoubtedly, as parents in the 21st century, we may ask if the Bible is proposing a prescriptive approach to discipline that involves some form of spanking. We wrestle with the decision of whether or not we will include this type of discipline in our homes. Some discourage this approach, and others promote it. And in the end, we can be left feeling confused and conflicted.

When it comes to discipline, it is more helpful to consider the principles found in Scripture than to seek a prescriptive approach. This is because any sort of methodology is powerless to change hearts, and ultimately, that is what we are after — our children turning away from sin and turning toward the things of God because of hearts transformed by the gospel. God desires repentance! So as moms, we want to see how and why God disciplines His children in Scripture.

We also want to consider other values that disciplining our children communicates. An important lesson we want our children to understand and embrace is the value of authority. Our God is a God of order, and when we exercise appropriate authority over our children and teach them to respect and embrace our authority, we are imaging God by bringing order to our homes. The purpose of the order in God's design is to bring peace and flourishing. Likewise, we can cultivate orderly homes that value love and respect to foster an atmosphere of peace and growth. When our children taste this kind of authority, they will not negatively view submission. They will be more likely to embrace the gift of boundaries, knowing it is for their good.

When it comes to enforcing discipline or teaching our children anything, how we communicate is incredibly powerful. In essence, our tone of voice, our body language, and our facial expressions say just as much as the actual words we use. While yelling may produce immediate results, it is communicating a lot more than we may intend to our children. Our exasperated sighs can communicate that they are an inconvenience and be a source of shame. Our yelling may communicate that we value our timeline above all else, and we are content using fear as a motivation for compliance. Ultimately, we can find ourselves communicating a message contrary to the gospel and misrepresenting the character and plan of God. Thus, whatever methodology we use, we want to ensure that the overall lesson of every disciplinary event is the gospel, pointing to the enduring, life-transforming gift of God's grace. And we want to be mindful that the way the lesson is delivered affirms the character of God as revealed in Scripture.

This does not mean we mince our words or shy away from presenting the whole gospel. Even for very young children, we can introduce the language of the Bible. When they do things out of their sinful nature, we call it what it is: sin. We teach them that our sin creates a divide between us and our holy God. This is the bad news that shows our children their need for Jesus. This means that every time they fall short, we offer them a taste of the good news of the gospel. We point them to Christ and His grace. We can communicate the seriousness of sin without encouraging shame when we make the gospel the only resolution to their sin problem. And we can communicate this with kindness. Being an ambassador of Christ, we follow His example and allow kindness to lead our children to repentance.

As moms, we have the opportunity to preach the gospel to our children daily and teach them that the gospel transforms us. When we put our faith in Christ, we are made new creations. We are empowered by the Spirit to fight our sin. Our obedience and good works are done in response to the gospel; it is never a means to receive forgiveness, acceptance, or favor. This leads us to freedom. We do not have to hide our messes, but we can confess our sins to one another and find Jesus enough for all of us.

Note: If you are seeking a more practical disciplinary method to use, seek out a mentor in your local church! Ask someone to walk alongside you in developing a method that clearly and consistently communicates the gospel to your children. We do not have to do this alone.

SCRIPTURE TO MEDITATE ON

Hebrews 12:7-11

QUESTIONS TO CONSIDER TO PROMPT PRAYER

How do you discipline your children? What does your approach communicate with your children? How can you communicate the gospel to your children even in times of discipline? Take some time to pray. Confess any sins if necessary.

Our obedience and good works are done in response to the gospel; it is never a means to receive forgiveness, acceptance, or favor.

"

As moms, we have the opportunity to preach the gospel to our children daily and teach them that the gospel transforms us.

WE HELP EACH OTHER GROW IN
OUR ABILITY TO APPLY THE GOSPEL
TO EVERY ASPECT OF OUR LIVES.

13

Does it Take a Village?

The Christian life was never meant to be lived out in isolation. Over and over again, we see in Scripture that God relates to His people individually and corporately. While He knows and calls us each by name, He then knits us into the body of Christ (1 Corinthians 12). He appoints us as "good stewards of the varied grace of God," entrusting to us specific gifts to benefit the common good (1 Peter 4:10). This reality impacts how we parent. As believers, we do not have to raise our children in isolation; we have the body of Christ to help us.

In Deuteronomy 6:4-9, we see that our personal devotion and faith in God precedes the command to pass it along to our children. As parents, we are to first know and love God with all of our heart, soul, mind, and strength. We are to treasure His Word and in turn be transformed by it. Part of this transformation is responding to the truth that when we are saved, we are not only saved from our sins but saved into a covenant community. We are now a part of the people of God, and we live this out in the context of the local church. Being a member of a local church is not just something Christians do; it is an essential component of living as new creations in Christ!

As believers, we understand that we need fellow believers to grow in Christlikeness. We need the local church to grow in our knowledge and love for God. This is why we regularly sit under the teaching and preaching of His Word. God has given us the gift of pastors to help us rightly handle the Word of God. We also study Scripture with others, welcoming them into our sanctification as they help us identify blind spots and sin patterns. We employ our spiritual gifts to benefit the body, and in turn, we receive the blessings of the giftings of others. This way of living is an outworking of the gospel.

This is why believers embrace a communal mindset to parenthood. This perspective is not the same as our culture's idea that it takes a village. We do not believe that all our children's needs can and should be met by society. As believers, we assume the primary responsibility of raising our children, but we invite the local church's influence on our family discipleship. We welcome the instruction and accountability of fellow believers with whom we are united in Christ. As fellow members of God's household, we share deep beliefs and convictions that are informed by God's Word. We agree that the end goal of all of life (parenthood included) is to glorify God, and we help each other to that end. This is the beauty of Christian mentorship. We help each other grow in our ability to apply the gospel to every aspect of our lives.

Raising disciples is messy and hard. Cultivating a gospel-saturated atmosphere at home is not an exact science. Engaging in family worship can feel impossible at times. As parents, we can often feel inadequate and unable to fulfill the responsibility of showing our children the character of God and teaching them the beauty of His commands. But rather than looking for ways to outsource or skirt around this God-given responsibility, we can look to the family of God for help. The gospel reminds us that we are needy, imperfect people. We do not have to hide the ugly parts of our parenting journeys from one another. We can confess our sins to one another. We can share our needs, both tangible and spiritual, and have them met both practically and prayerfully.

In the end, this is a gift to our children. When our families are active in the local church, we are organically teaching our children the communal aspect of our union with Christ. We are allowing them to see the gospel more fully on display through the church. As they interact with and learn from other believers, they have the opportunity to more clearly see the fullness of God. They can experience the unifying power of the gospel in the church's diversity in real-time. Rather than saying it takes a village, let us change the narrative to be that it takes a church.

SCRIPTURE TO MEDITATE ON

Deuteronomy 6:4-9, 1 Corinthians 12:4-7

QUESTIONS TO CONSIDER TO PROMPT PRAYER

What role does the local church have in your life? How could you invite fellow believers into your parenting journey? What could the local church teach your children that you cannot teach them on your own? Take some time to pray. Confess any sins, if necessary.

ULTIMATELY, WE TRUST THE
LORD IN ALL THINGS.

14

Personal Conscience

Many of us have like-minded mom friends who we frequently consult about all things motherhood. It is a gift to have these kindred spirits who can walk alongside us in our journeys. As moms, we have so many decisions to make, and these decisions seem to become more and more complex as time goes on. It is helpful to give and receive input from trusted friends to make informed decisions. However, we quickly realize that no two persons fully agree on every single issue out there. No two women will mother the same way.

There are many reasons for this, but above all, God made us as unique individuals. Every single person on this planet has his or her own unique fingerprint, even identical twins! While they share the same DNA, their fingerprints are distinct. They have their own personalities, interests, and talents. No one is a perfect carbon copy of another. We are our own persons, and our individuality is compounded by our unique cultural backgrounds, family upbringings, and life experiences. And by God's good design, no two persons have the same conscience.

It is our conscience guiding us as we navigate the gray areas of life. It is our individual sense of right and wrong, and it is a capacity that is given to us by God. While some may despise the conscience, it is a gift from God for our protection. This does not mean that our consciences are perfect; no, even as believers, our consciences do not perfectly align with God's will and law. However, they can be informed and shaped by God's Word to make moral judgments reflecting the character and value of God.

This is a lifelong process. In God's wisdom, He made us diverse, and He uses our diversity to continue His mission. A powerful reality of the gospel is that it produces unity in diversity, but this unity does not imply uniformity. It transcends generational, racial, cultural, political, financial, and social differences. It gathers diverse people under the Word of God, where believers collectively uphold Scripture as the authority on absolute truth. We believe the Bible is sufficient, but it will not answer every single question we have in black and white.

There are many decisions we have to make that remain in the gray areas of Scripture. This implies that there is Christian liberty. As believers, we are free to use wisdom in moving forward in these areas. Our consciences will help us navigate these areas of Christian freedom and answer questions like:

> *How do you deal with sleep regressions?*
> *What tricks do you use for picky eaters?*
> *What does character training look like?*
> *How do you navigate screen time?*
> *What schooling option do you prefer?*
> *How can we practice rhythms of rest with babies and toddlers?*
> *What potty-training method is best?*

We can consult with trusted friends and mentors regarding these matters to help us in our parenting journeys. As we agree on the primary issues of the Christian faith which are clear in Scripture, we extend grace to one another in the others. We help one another determine how the gospel applies to the different areas of life, but we embrace the gift of personal conscience.

Ultimately, we trust the Lord in all things. We seek His Word for counsel and wisdom. We commune with Him in prayer. We strive to be of one accord with our spouses. We submit our consciences to the Lord and ask Him to align us to Himself. And while we do this, we invite our children into the process. While our children's salvation is ultimately the work of the Lord, we faithfully present God's Word before them, allowing it to shape their consciences too.

SCRIPTURE TO MEDITATE ON

Romans 14:13-19

QUESTIONS TO CONSIDER TO PROMPT PRAYER

*What has shaped your conscience? To what extent does Bible intake
inform and shape your conscience today? What gray areas in Scripture
do you wrestle with regarding motherhood? Take some time to pray.
Confess any sins if necessary.*

OUR WORDS AND ACTIONS CAN
CULTIVATE A GOSPEL-SATURATED
ATMOSPHERE IN OUR HOMES.

15

The Power of Words

Our actions can loudly project our thoughts, values, and character. However, our words do too. When we go to Scripture, we see a tremendous emphasis on the power of words. Proverbs 12:18 says, "There is one who speaks rashly, like a piercing sword." Those of us who have wielded words to hurt others know this well. Or maybe we have witnessed how a harsh word crushes a child's spirit. The words that come from our mouths are powerful—to either build up or tear down. And when we look at Scripture, we see that it was God's design to embed such power and importance in words.

Scripture tells us that our salvation is brought forth by the Word of Truth. Romans 10:17 says, "So faith comes from what is heard, and what is heard comes through the message about Christ" (also see James 1:18). The transmission of the gospel requires the use of words. This is why we cannot solely rely on our actions to share the good news of Jesus Christ. We have to use real words, too!

This has tremendous implications for us as mothers. While we cannot guarantee our children's salvation by our actions and words, we can be mindful of how we live and speak to communicate the life-giving beauty of the gospel to our families. Our words and actions can cultivate a gospel-saturated atmosphere in our homes. And the truth is, we have countless opportunities every single day to do this. Consider these statistics: on average, men and women speak 16,000 words a day, and preschoolers hear up to 21,000 words in a single day! So we have to ask ourselves what we are saying. What are our children hearing? Are we communicating in such a way as to magnify the gospel?

We cannot do this on our own. Scripture tells us that we cannot tame our tongues (James 3:8). The entire third chapter of the book of James uses the tongue as a primary representation for the whole of human depravity. This is because words are reliable indicators of the condition of one's heart. Jesus taught this in Matthew 12:34b when He said, "For the mouth speaks from the overflow of the heart." All of us have spoken in anger. We have participated in gossip. We have used words to intentionally cause harm. Our words have shown us that we are sinners in need of a Savior. The sin of speech is a universal problem, and the only real hope for any of us is the gospel.

This is why we do not lose heart. As redeemed sinners, we are transformed by the gospel. We are not hopeless, and we want to use our words to communicate the glorious truth to our kids—that in Christ, there is hope! They have dignity as image-bearers of God. While they are sinners, there is One who has come to redeem them from their depravity. As moms, we wisely choose our words to regularly communicate timeless truths found in the Bible. We teach them what Scripture declares as true and untrue. We saturate our words with grace, extending kindness to lead our children to repentance. Our choice of words, tone of voice, and use of sighs can either affirm the gospel and reflect the character of God or contradict them.

We need the Spirit to do this. Motherhood is exhausting, and our flesh wants to take the path of least resistance to produce results. So we yell or use threatening words or a harsh tone to get the response we desire. However, Jesus has broken the power of sin in our lives. We are invited to rely on the Spirit's empowering to say no to our flesh and tame our tongues. We go to the Word and allow it to sanctify us (John 17:17). We fill our hearts with the promises of God and allow that to overflow into what we say and how we say it. We go to the Lord in prayer in repentance and giving praise. We ask the Spirit to help us heed God's Word which calls us to use words to build others up (Ephesians 4:29) and always speak graciously (Colossians 4:6).

Our words are powerful in shaping our children and their views of themselves, the world, and God. May we speak in such a way that reflects the gentleness of Christ. And may we remember that one day, each of us will give an account of "every careless word" we speak (Matthew 12:36).

SCRIPTURE TO MEDITATE ON

Ephesians 4:29, Matthew 12:36

QUESTIONS TO CONSIDER TO PROMPT PRAYER

What do your words and the way you speak them say about the state of your heart? Do your words toward your spouse and your children primarily build up or tear down? Take some time to pray. Confess any sins if necessary.

OUR STRUGGLE WITH
EMOTIONS REVEALS OUR
NEED FOR A SAVIOR.

16

Emotions

Our culture tells us that women are emotional creatures, and there seems to be a negative connotation to this. Many of us do not want to be emotional or deep feelers. Yet, in Scripture, we see that God made His image-bearers to be emotional beings. We were created to feel. God has gifted us with emotions. However, many of our feelings (fear of man, shame, rage, etc.) remind us that our emotions are distorted due to the fall. We wonder if we should trust our emotions or if there is a healthy way to engage our feelings.

These are important things to consider. As moms, we feel many things. Our love for our children runs deeply, driving us to feel joyous, protective, cautious, overwhelmed, proud, worried, and a host of other emotions. The complexity of our emotions can be compounded by our hormones, life circumstances, or even our diets. So while it is true that we should not always trust our feelings, it is wise for each of us to evaluate them regularly. Our emotions are valuable because they tell us a lot about what we believe to be true and valuable. They reveal what is going on in our hearts. The goal is not to reject our feelings; instead, we strive to engage our feelings in a healthy, God-honoring way.

How do we do this? We have to slow down and be honest with ourselves. If we are feeling overwhelmed or burned out, it could be because we are failing to rest. But it also reveals our hearts. We may not believe that God is trustworthy to be in control. If we are feeling insecure, it could mean we are failing to believe that our identities are in Christ alone. Perhaps we are idolizing our bodies or our reputations. We must do the hard work of identifying our emotions and bringing them before the Lord. Knowing our feelings are often fleeting, we have to take it to the one constant thing: the Bible. It is His Word that tells us what is true, and that is what we should want to believe and value. We, as His image-bearers, should want to love what God loves and hate what He hates, and we are told this in His Word. We can and should rejoice, mourn, grieve, and delight as He does.

This is crucial for us to do as mothers because how we engage our emotions profoundly impacts our families. For better or for worse, our emotional states as moms can set the tone in our homes. But more than that, we are teaching our children the purpose and value of emotions. If we do not want our children to be mastered by their feelings, we cannot be mastered by our feelings. If we want our children to uphold God's Word as the standard of truth—not their feelings—then we need to do the same. We can model for our children what it looks like to allow Scripture to inform and shape how we feel and respond to all aspects of life.

One emotion we can do this with is anger. Many of us quickly deem anger as a bad emotion. We shy away from feeling any sort of anger because we think all anger is sinful. However, remember that God displayed anger in Scripture without compromising His holiness. This is righteous anger. He hates sin, and He feels anger over its effects. Likewise, it is right for us to feel anger over the injustices of this world caused by sin. We should want our children to feel anger and godly grief over sin as well. We do not want to label emotions as good or bad; instead, we can live our emotions out in a healthy way.

We will not do this perfectly. There will be moments when we are experiencing sinful anger, discontentment, anxiety, jealousy, or other emotions. There will be moments when our children are throwing tantrums and are overwhelmed by their feelings. These are simply opportunities to preach the gospel to ourselves and our children. Our struggle with emotions reveals our need for a Savior. We acknowledge that our hearts are prone to wander. We are forgetful beings. But we have a Good Shepherd who leads us. We have His Word, His Spirit, and His people to help us. We do not need to depend on positive self-talk, suppress our feelings, or pretend that everything is okay. There is a better way, and that is to seek the Lord and allow Him to transform our hearts and minds. Our emotions can lead us to truth, love, and worship.

SCRIPTURE TO MEDITATE ON

Ephesians 4:26-27, Philippians 4:4-7

QUESTIONS TO CONSIDER TO PROMPT PRAYER

What is your current emotional state? What do your emotions tell you about what your heart currently believes to be true? What are the main emotions expressed by your children, and what does that tell you about their hearts? What can you personally do to teach your children to engage their emotions in a healthy, God-honoring way? Take some time to pray. Confess any sins if necessary.

"

We can model for
our children what it looks
like to allow Scripture to
inform and shape how we
feel and respond to
all aspects of life.

Thank you for studying
God's Word with us!

CONNECT WITH US

@thedailygraceco
@kristinschmucker

CONTACT US

info@thedailygraceco.com

SHARE

#thedailygraceco
#lampandlight

VISIT US ONLINE

thedailygraceco.com

MORE DAILY GRACE

The Daily Grace App
Daily Grace Podcast